I0421669

Where's Your Head At?

A self-help guide

to understanding your mind.

by Mark Cresswell B.Beh.Sci.,
B.A.Hons., (psych), M.Ed.,
MCPCA.,FAACP.

.

ISBN: 978-0-6486605-1-4 (paperback)

Cataloguing-in-publication information for
this title is listed with the National Library of
Australia.

Published in Australia by
Cockatoo Gate Publishing.

cockatoog8@gmail.com

Where's Your Head At?

This book is intended to guide you on an amazing journey. The journey involves looking within yourself and into your mind— the most incredible place on the planet and probably in the universe.

When I considered a title for this book, I was tempted to call it "Here Be Monsters". On old mariners charts you may see that appellation where the waters were uncharted, often accompanied by drawings of mythical beasts like Krakens and Dragons.

When we consider the mind and its relationship to our behaviours, it becomes clear there are indeed monsters lurking in the depths. This book will, I hope, give you the skills and confidence to confront those monsters and drive them out, or at least tame them enough to make them acceptable house guests.

Mark Cresswell

How to use this Guide

Questions—these are here to guide your self-analysis. The more honestly you answer, the more complete will be the process of change. You may not know the 'real' answer to a question, but your first, best answer will be a start on the road to your truth.

Affirmations- these are here to give you ways to replace negative or intrusive thoughts. It is not uncommon to have negative thoughts in our daily lives. Carry the affirmations. You can choose one for the day or pick the affirmation to suit the situation. Practice using them. It takes work to drown out intrusive thoughts, so keep the affirmations close (on your mirror or computer, in your wallet) and refer to them when needed.

The Epiphany or Moment of Clarity

Regardless of the reason for our problems or the length of time we carry them, there will come a time when we have a sudden insight into our behaviours and a desire to stop whatever we are doing.

This is often called the Moment of Clarity. You may hear the alcoholic/addict call it, "The time when you are sick and tired of being sick and tired".

What happened to get me here?

For example:

1/ Waking up in the morning not remembering or regretting behaviours of the previous night.

2/ Reacting angrily to a suggestion for improvement at work

What stops me from moving from here?

Example:

1/ I am afraid to give up my coping behaviours – what if the change is worse?

2/ What if the suggestion was right and I am not as good at my job as I thought I was?

Where do I want to get to?

Example:

1/ I want to be able to live without engaging in risky behaviours

2/ I want to be recognised as doing a good job/ knowing my job

----

If nothing changes, nothing changes.

Why are you reading this? Do you desire change?

Reading this won't make the changes. Action makes change. Act to change your thinking and behaviours. People read self-help books all the time. Is reading the book a change? NO! Change takes time, commitment, and practice.

If you don't do the exercises and don't examine your beliefs and behaviours, nothing will change. And if nothing changes, nothing changes. There is a saying that the definition of insanity is doing the same thing over and over, expecting a different outcome.

Do something different—it may not work but it will surely produce a different outcome, and this is what produces personal growth. Even if you don't like the outcome you will learn from it, and it may give you clues to determining your next action.

I am reminded of the old joke—How many psychologists does it take to change a lightbulb? —Just one, but the lightbulb has really got to want to change.

There is some truth in this. You must really want to change. Why? Because change is hard. If it was easy, we would all have done it yesterday.

Change takes effort and commitment. Sometimes we put in less or more effort and sometimes the commitment will waver.

What do I need to do?

Example:

1/ I need to develop different coping mechanisms

2/ I need to control my anger

What can I do now?

Example:

1/ Learn about what causes my need for negative coping mechanisms

2/ Learn about what causes my anger

What do you want to be when you grow up?

This is all about identity. Who are you? How do others see you?

This is your opportunity to reshape yourself to the person you want to be. But be prepared. Whatever changes you make, others may not like it. Remember, they have been relating to you as you are for a long time. Whether the changes are physical or emotional, you may have to re-educate them to see the new you.

Some people will not like the changes, others will embrace them. This is all about you. You do not have any responsibility to anyone except yourself.

You get to decide the rest of your life and those that want to come along for the ride will do so. You cannot and must not be held back by the naysayers. They do not have your interests at heart. They are fearful of change and unsure of their position in the new order. Let them work it out for themselves.

What do I want to be when I grow up?

Example:

1/ I want to be in control of my emotions/needs

2/ I want to be seen as competent

Personal Responsibility

If you are over 18 in Australia (or whatever legal age it may be in your country) you are an adult and you are responsible for your actions.

I understand you may have had a shitty life, and you may have been subject to appalling things. This may have influenced how you relate to others and your lifestyle.

It does not, however, absolve you of responsibility for seeking help.

No one can make you do, say, think or feel anything that you don't want to do. You may react to anger by feeling guilty or sad, but it's not the other person making you feel bad, it's you.

I know this is a hard concept to grasp (and so early in the book), and a challenging one.

Let us look at an example:

Someone is robbing your store, puts a gun to your head, and tells you to open the safe. You have a choice—to open the safe or not. It is a shitty choice, but still, yours to make.

If someone gives you a cake and tells you to eat it, it is your choice to make!

What am I doing now? (e.g., I'm drinking beer.)

Why am I doing it? (e.g., I feel bad about something.)

What made me feel bad? (e.g., Someone did or said something or I did something 'wrong'.)

This is my feeling, and I am responsible. (Just because this thing happened doesn't mean I have to feel bad—I can choose my emotions.)

Self Esteem

How often do we notice our feelings of self-worth are related to the behaviours we have demonstrated recently? As previously discussed, this is related to our beliefs. If we believe that we must behave in certain ways and don't behave that way, that impacts our self-esteem negatively.

What if we were able to separate the person from the behaviour? What if it didn't matter how you behaved in order to feel good about yourself (or other people, for that matter)?

This is a difficult concept for many to grasp. There are two factors to consider:

The person as an entity, and

The behaviour as a separate entity.

If your child deliberately spills their food or hits someone, does that make them a bad child. Most people would say no, what they did was bad, but they are still just a child and not a bad person.

Does the child feel inherently bad for engaging in this behaviour? Clearly not, the child only begins to feel bad when scolded and told they are bad.

AFFIRMATIONS

The following pages contain affirmations. Cut them out, pin them up and recite them daily.

CAREER

Goal: *Know that what you are doing is worthwhile; you are valuable*

I am valuable; I am appreciated; My work is important.

I love the work I do; What's next?! (Yeah!!).

I am always productive; Success comes easily to me.

I begin this day with confidence; I am me regardless of what I do.

My team is qualified and capable; Our clients are happy and satisfied.

I believe in our products and services; I am rewarded for all the work I do.

As I succeed, I become more lovable; The Universe supports my every effort.

My work is always recognised positively.

I deserve to be successful doing work I love; It's okay to be peaceful and ambitious at the same time.

I take myself lightly while I take my work in life seriously.

Every task I do is worthwhile and is part of a bigger plan.

I respect my abilities and always work to my full potential.

SELF-ESTEEM

Goal: _Shine with inner knowledge that you are truly wonderful._

I am valuable; I am intelligent.

I walk in beauty.

I never give up; I can do anything.

I accept myself as I am; I respect myself.

I am as free as a bird.

I am free to be myself.

I am good, and I know it.

I am a talented person.

I have confidence in myself.

I am captain of my ship.

My heart is open and ready.

I deserve to be treated right.

✂ I am a success in all that I do.

I pay more attention to myself.

I am achieving all my goals.

I believe in my gifts and abilities.

I release my need to be humiliated.

I release my habit of self-criticism.

Every choice I make is the right one.

My own expectations are exceeded.

My insecurity is replaced with wisdom.

At my centre is an incandescent fire.

I release myself from harmful judgments.

My existence is important to the Universe.

I'm the best thing that's ever happened to me.

LOVE
<u>*Goal:*</u> *Love without fear, love as you would be loved*

I live in love.

I fly with love.

I love without fear.

I speak my needs.

I am worthy of love.

Wherever I go, I am loved.

There is purity in the quiet touch.

Love is eternal and everlasting.

Love flows into my life like a river.

I am a magnet to loving relationships.

I allow myself to receive love without guilt.

My relationships make perfect sense to me.

My partner is understanding and supportive.

I accept others as they are, just as they accept me.

The more I love, the more that love is returned to me.

HEALTH & WELL-BEING
Goal: Your body is a temple; enjoy vitality

I am joyful.

I am letting go.

My mind is at peace.

I am healthy and happy.

I feel absolutely supercharged.

I am welcoming peace.

I allow myself to be quiet.

I am at peace with myself.

Today is my chance to be healthy.

My vital energy resurfaces naturally.

I enjoy the food that is good for me.

I am healthy in all aspects of my being.

I have the power to control my health.

I am in control of my health and wellness.

I am always able to maintain my ideal weight.

I always treat my body with love and respect.

I have abundant energy, vitality, and well-being.

I am filled with energy to do all the daily activities in my life.

EMOTIONS

Goal: Learn to release emotions, lighten up

I am letting go of anger.

I welcome forgiveness.

I am a forgiving and loving person.

I deserve to be free from guilt.

I am blameless for another person's anger.

I am honest and truthful in all I say and do.

My strength comes from forgiveness of myself and others.

I always maintain the power I need to be positive and have joy.

MOVING ON
Goal: _Look forward to the new joy each moment without baggage brings_

I give closure to the past; I cut the cords that bind me.

I deserve to fulfil my destiny.

I adjust to change in my life.

I welcome change in my life.

My future is full of possibilities.

I invite new choices into my life.

I live free from struggle and fear.

I seek and find what I need within me.

I release my need to deaden my feelings.

Change in my life is a way for me to learn.

The plan of my life reveals itself naturally.

New realms of possibility gleam before me.

I accept peace and joy in all aspects of my life.

I learn valuable lessons from change in my life.

I am in control of my life by the choices I make.

I'm ready to live life to its fullest, and life's ready for me.

I nurture my inner child, love her, and have allowed her to heal.

I make every act an act of love, freedom, mastery, and hope.

Shit Happens

Yes, it does. Shit Happens! Shit Happens Randomly! Shit Happens to Good People!

Get used to it. You are not in control of the universe. You cannot control the actions of others. You can only control yourself. So, when shit happens to you, you can choose to get down and relapse, or you can suck it up—Accept that it didn't happen because you are a bad person or did something to deserve it. It just happened.

You only need to accept responsibility for the things you can control and the things you can change. The rest is not your concern. Allow yourself the flexibility to move with the changes around you, to let the universe wash over you. Bend like a willow instead of standing strong and rigid until you break.

What happened?

Example:

I had an argument with my partner.

_____
_____
_____
_____
_____
_____
_____
_____
_____
_____
_____
_____
_____
_____
_____

Is this beyond my personal control?

Example- Yes and no. I can't control what my partner says and does but I can control how I respond.

How will I change the way I react to it?

Example:

I could listen and only respond when I am sure of the issue. I could respond and own how I feel.

Wherever you go, there you are.

A statement of the obvious? If so, why is it that people will choose to run away from their problems, leave town, leave jobs, leave family, rather than confront the issues?

If you are miserable here, be assured you will be miserable somewhere else. Sometimes we make a change, and everything seems to be better. This is usually the result of the excitement of change itself. New people, new places take our attention away from our problems for a while and make it seem as if all is well.

It will come back and bite you (you know where) when you least expect it. As soon as you are settled in and life seems to be going fine, the old problems will resurface.

Who am I really?

For example- I am an anxious person

Is this who I want to be? What is it about me I don't like?

For example-my anxiety stops me leaving the house

Who do I want to be?

Who's Driving Your Bus'?

If you were stepping on to a bus and the driver was clearly under the influence of drugs or alcohol, would you get on?

How often do we tell our children, "Don't get into a car with a driver who has been drinking".

And yet, we get onto a bus every day with a driver who is out of control. YOU!

If you are not in control of your desires and demons, what is likely to happen? The driver of the bus will crash you straight into the thing you are trying to avoid.

"Ah," I hear you say, "this is about will power."

NO

This is about WON'T power. Won't power comes from <u>understanding your desires and drives</u>. Will power is simply the ability to avoid something.

Won't power requires you to understand what is pushing you and to actively take steps to control that desire.

"How do I do that?" I hear you ask.

Analyse your belief system.

All our behaviours are driven by our beliefs about ourselves and about the world around us. These can be so deep-seated as to act upon us without us even being aware of their existence.

Let us look at the ABC of beliefs:

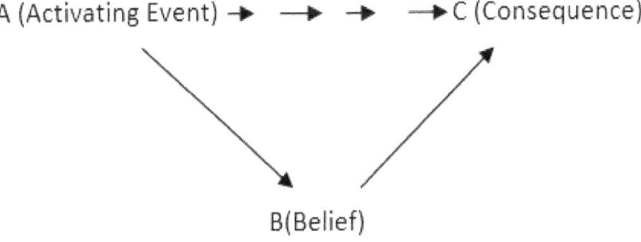

Generally, people believe something happens (an Activating event), and then there is a Consequence (the path of the 4 horizontal arrows above).

For example: Someone cuts you off on the roundabout (event), and you get angry (consequence).

This is not what happens. All our experiences are channelled through our belief system (unbroken diagonal arrows on diagram above). This happens so quickly that it is instantaneous and therefore difficult (but not impossible), to analyse.

For example: Someone cuts you off on the roundabout (event). You believe the person is ignorant, a bad driver, and shouldn't be allowed on the road (belief). You get angry (consequence).

So, it pays to analyse our beliefs. When we do that, we can see the ones that cause an emotional response are irrational. By that, I mean the ones that contain <u>absolute statements</u>, and so are impossible to live up to.

Absolute Statements contain words like:

Must

Should

Have to

Ought to

Always

Never

We call this Musterbating!

These statements will simply set you up to fail.

Example: I have to keep the house clean.

Really? Why? And what happens the first time you don't clean the house? You feel guilty.

What would happen if you didn't clean the house?

The Critical Question

There is a question I like to ask myself whenever I feel driven to do something, or if I am not wanting to do something.

Will I die from this?

Is the decision I am about to make a threat to life and limb—If it is, then don't do it. If it isn't—what am I worried about?

So:

What would happen if you didn't clean the house?

Let us analyse the belief.

Action	Clean the house
Belief	I should have a clean house.
Underlying irrational statement	A good mother always keeps the house clean.
Emotional response to non-compliance	I feel guilty for not behaving how I'm supposed to.
Modified Rational Statement	It would be nice to have a clean house but sometimes life gets in the way and that is okay. It will not harm anything to leave the house uncleaned today.
New Emotional response	I feel okay.

Action	
Belief	
Underlying irrational statement	
Emotional response to non-compliance	
Modified Rational Statement	
New Emotional response	

There are many irrational beliefs. In fact, our lives are built on them, and as a result, our behaviours are driven by them. The first step in gaining control of our emotions, and thus our behaviours, is to analyse our beliefs.

You can use the table above, or copy it, to do this. You might want to start with some simple ones like cleaning the house, preparing meals, or our friend on the roundabout.

Sometimes it is hard to analyse our beliefs and to confront the irrational nature of them. Sometimes we want to keep our beliefs. That is okay. Remember what was said earlier—You are an adult, and you are responsible for your emotions, beliefs, and behaviours. So, if you want to keep an irrational belief, that is okay, but you must be prepared to accept the emotional response that comes whenever that belief is triggered by an activating event.

When setting goals, we must remember the SMART principals.

Specific. Goals must deal with something tangible. A goal is not 'I want to be happy'. A goal might be 'I want to find a better job (which might help me to feel happier)'.

Measurable. The measure of wanting a new job is in being offered one. The search for a new job does not measure the goal. You could break the goal down into smaller goals such as— 'I will apply for 3 jobs a week'.

Achievable. The goal of getting a new job may not be achievable because it is somewhat out of your control. On the other hand, the smaller goal of applying for jobs is achievable because it is entirely in your realm of control.

Realistic. Getting a new job may be realistic (certainly the goal of applying is), but it will depend largely on the final factor as to the likelihood of a positive outcome.

Timely. Do I want to achieve a new job tomorrow or within 12 months? The timing of your goals must reflect the level of difficulty likely to be encountered in achieving them. At the same time, the timeframe must be short enough to provide a level of motivation. If you say you want to get a new job in 10 years, there is no motivation to change.

When we talk about goals in our daily life, we often mean dreams. It is important to write down your goals (use the template provided below or copy it), and to keep them where you will be able to review them regularly. Don't be afraid to modify or remove a goal. Goals are not an end in themselves. They are a means to achieve focus. The focus you have today may not be tomorrows. This does not mean that you should discard goals willy-nilly. Just because you have not achieved a goal by the time you wanted, does not automatically make that goal invalid.

Review the goal honestly and determine if it is still a valid goal. If it can still be put into the template, and the SMART process is met, then it is still valid. Sometimes we underestimate the time needed to achieve things. Sometimes we must change course for a while or break the goal into smaller pieces. These are all valid approaches.

Specific	Nominate something that can be actioned	Example: To save $500 for Christmas presents
Measurable	Will I be able to test that I am achieving something (size, shape, amount)?	There will be $500 in my account
Achievable	Can I reach this goal? Not a chance— remove it. 50/50—give it a shot. Absolutely—high priority	I can save this amount
Realistic	Is it within my power?	I will not struggle with this amount
Timely	Timeframe Short term: 1–6 months Medium term: 6–12 months Long term: over 12 months	I can do it regularly and in time
Outcome Review Date	Date to be achieved	24/12/2021

Specific	Nominate something that can be actioned	Your Goal:
Measurable	Will I be able to test that I am achieving something (size, shape, amount)?	
Achievable	Can I reach this goal? Not a chance— remove it. 50/50—give it a shot. Absolutely—high priority	
Realistic	Is it within my power?	
Timely	Timeframe Short term: 1–6 months Medium term: 6–12 months Long term: over 12 months	
Outcome Review Date	Date to be achieved	

Don't 'Give Up'

A chapter with dual meaning.

Of course, we all know that to succeed at something we should try and try again. An initial failure is not an indicator of ultimate success or failure. The same is true of an initial success. Relapse is possible but not inevitable. You may experience your epiphany and go from strength to strength without falling. Why would you question that? Why would you place doubts in your own mind? Why would you expect relapse?

Take the success and go with it. Remember to always be mindful. Relapse happens when we forget the lessons we have learned, when we stop consciously analysing our beliefs and behaviours. If we slip into unconscious patterns, we are more likely to allow the old beliefs and behaviours to resurface.

The second meaning.

Why must we 'give up' something to get better? Did you give up drinking, smoking, or chocolate? If you are overweight, should you give up food? All these things imply deprivation. "I have had to give up something I love in order to regain my life."

Change your thoughts, rewrite your scripts.

Smoking— "I am a non-smoker."

Drinking— "I am a non-drinker."

Weight— "I eat only healthy foods."

Note how these are all positive and immediate statements. They affirm the individual choice. They clearly show that the person is living in the now. You do not have to be concerned with what you once did. It is what you do now that is important. See yourself as that person now, use a script that affirms who you are now.

Who am I right now?

Games People Play

Let us assume for a moment that William Shakespeare was right when he wrote:

"All the world's a stage. And all the men and women merely players. They have their exits and their entrances. And one man in his time plays many parts…"

Let us compare acting with game playing. We have a role and if we perform that role correctly, we get rewarded. With acting we get applause (maybe an Oscar), and with games we score points and maybe even win.

Life, like games, is all about points. We play our particular games and roles, and we perform particular behaviours for a reason. That reason is to gain points. Points are simply a reward of some sort. We repeat the behaviours because they are reinforced, that is we keep getting points. For the poorly behaved child, those points could simply be the attention of a parent. As adults we often ignore the reason we behave in particular ways. It makes sense, therefore, to analyse why we do things. To look at the points we are trying to gain from those behaviours.

Once we have worked that out, it is then possible to determine if we want to continue trying to score those points or if we want to change our behaviours.

This brings us to Guilt. It is one of those emotions which has absolutely no redeeming features.

Why do we feel guilty? We feel guilty because we are not playing by the rules of our game, whatever that game may be. If you identify the rules of your game and can see you are not following the rules, there is a solution which will resolve your guilt.

Play by the rules or change the game.

Most people choose to play by the rules even if it is painful. Why?

Because if change were easy, we would have done it yesterday. Change is difficult, often painful, and often results in unforeseen upheaval. "Why then," you ask, "would we change?" To change, you need to grow and expand your knowledge of yourself and others. It makes you a much more enlightened person. Importantly, though, you will find as you grow, that the need for and occurrence of guilt becomes diminished to nothing.

What are my games?

What do I want from them?

How can I change the rules?